my itty-bitty bio

Connor McDavid

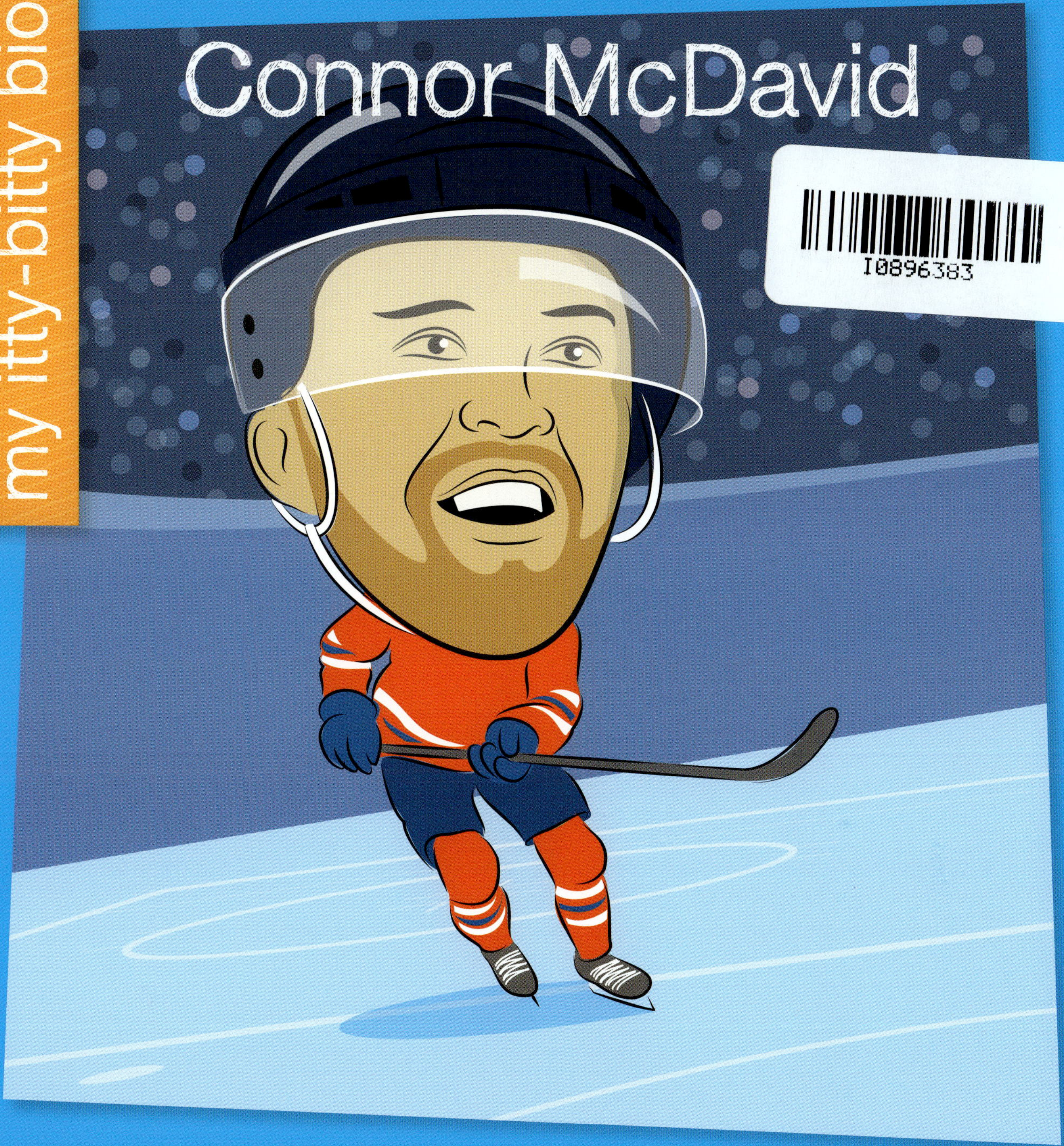

Cherry Lake Press

Published in the United States of America by Cherry Lake Publishing
Ann Arbor, Michigan
www.cherrylakepublishing.com

Reading Adviser: Marla Conn, MS, Ed., Literacy specialist, Read-Ability, Inc.
Book Designer: Jennifer Wahi
Illustrator: Jeff Bane

Photo Credits: © Inga Locmele/Shutterstock, 5; © Daniel Barry/Shutterstock, 7; © Arina P Habich/Shutterstock, 9; © Paul Mckinnon/Dreamstime.com, 11, 17; © Gints Ivuskans/Shutterstock, 13, 19, 22, 23; © Volkova Irina/Shutterstock, 15; © Connor Mah/Flickr, 21; Cover, 1, 6, 12, 16, Jeff Bane; Various frames throughout, © Shutterstock images

Cherry Lake Press is an imprint of Cherry Lake Publishing Group.

Library of Congress Cataloging-in-Publication Data

Names: Pincus, Meeg, author. | Bane, Jeff, 1957- illustrator.
Title: Connor McDavid / Meeg Pincus ; illustrated by Jeff Bane.
Description: Ann Arbor, Michigan : Cherry Lake Publishing, 2021. | Series: My itty-bitty bio | Includes index. | Audience: Grades K-1
Identifiers: LCCN 2020005536 (print) | LCCN 2020005537 (ebook) | ISBN 9781534168442 (hardcover) | ISBN 9781534170124 (paperback) | ISBN 9781534171961 (pdf) | ISBN 9781534173804 (ebook)
Subjects: LCSH: McDavid, Connor, 1997---Juvenile literature. | Hockey players--Canada--Biography--Juvenile literature.
Classification: LCC GV848.5.M395 P56 2021 (print) | LCC GV848.5.M395 (ebook) | DDC 796.962092 [B]--dc23
LC record available at https://lccn.loc.gov/2020005536
LC ebook record available at https://lccn.loc.gov/2020005537

Printed in the United States of America
Corporate Graphics

table of contents

About the author: Meeg Pincus has been a writer, editor, and educator for 25 years. She loves to write inspiring stories for kids about people, animals, and our planet. She lives near San Diego, California, where she enjoys the beach, reading, singing, and her family.

About the illustrator: Jeff Bane and his two business partners own a studio along the American River in Folsom, California, home of the 1849 Gold Rush. When Jeff's not sketching or illustrating for clients, he's either swimming or kayaking in the river to relax.

my story

I was born in Ontario, Canada.
It was 1997.

I have an older brother.

I always liked to play hockey.
I played as early as 3 years old.

What do you like to play?

I was a **rising star** in hockey. I was fast and strong. I played on teams with older kids.

VAUGHN
BAUER
Capitals

I was really good. I was allowed to play for the **OHL** at 15. Players had to be 16 to play. I was called the next Wayne Gretzky. He is considered the greatest hockey player ever!

ERIE
CCM

I was the first **draft pick** for **professional** hockey. I was 18.

ATVIJAS GĀZE

I got hurt in my first season. I missed 37 games. But I didn't let that stop me. I came back strong.

I won top **scorer** and fastest skater in pro hockey. My **fellow** players voted me best player.

ROGERS TV
McDAVID
97

I try to be a good leader. I became the youngest team **captain** ever in pro hockey.

What makes a good leader?

I am a young hockey star. I am a team leader. I **inspire** kids to chase their dreams.

What would you like to ask me?

2015

1990

Born 1997

2016

2090

glossary & index

glossary

captain (KAP-tuhn) the leader of a team

draft pick (DRAFT PIK) a player picked by a professional sports team at the only time teams are allowed to choose

fellow (FEL-oh) being in the same group, category, or situation

inspire (in-SPIRE) to fill someone with a feeling or idea

OHL (OH AYCH EL) Ontario Hockey League; it is one of the three major junior ice hockey leagues in Canada

professional (pruh-FESH-uh-nuhl) making money for working hard at something others do for fun

rising star (RIZE-ing STAHR) a person quickly moving up in position or rank in their field

scorer (SKOR-er) a person who makes a point or contest

index